Broken Boy

By Gavin Conroy

Dedicated to my transgender brothers and sisters who battle on the daily to survive. For those who have come out and those who live in the shadows— you are seen. You are loved. You are sacred. And you are not alone.

A Note From The Author

This is a collection of poetry. As a transman, I have a deep well of personal struggles and experiences that helped to craft these words. I have poured my heart into these pages and when you read it, you will see that the content can be dark, depending on the poem. The pain you will read is real and I want to warn the readers that it can be triggering. The following content references sexual abuse, religious abuse, transgender abuse, homophobia, struggles with identity, salvation, and suicide.

Please be cautious as you read.
I wanted to share my words
because so many of the other
humans on this planet share
my experience and are often
looking, as I have, for
someone else to validate that
experience. For someone else
to see that pain. I hope I
manage to connect with those
people.

THE PAIN OF REBIRTH

Heart Scream

I am a sail rippled wide by the
storm
A bird caught in the crosswind.
A spinning compass with no
arrow.

Directionless, frightened,
drowning.

I am the rain dripping down
the window.
The wailing cry of the wind in
the trees.
The ache beneath your
breastbone.

Ephemeral, empty, alone.

Broken Boy

I am the blood that runs.
The breath that chokes,
The heart that screams.

Vulnerable, soft, human.

I am a soul with hopes and
dreams.
A wish upon a star,
A kiss that never ends.

Wanderer, romantic,
deserving.

I am Gavin.
I am he.
I am him.
I am me.

Broken, flawed, trying.

Panic

This is panic in varying stages.
Cold and blunt.
Knife-like and cruel.
Debilitating and feral.

Harsh.
Critical.
Unkind and painful.

This is panic.
This is the fracturing of fear
into a thousand scurrying ants.
Intrepid little parasites of
courage, control, and calm.

They feed off the mind.

Clawing through the web of lies
that make a man—that BREAK
a man.
This is panic.

Broken Boy

Ache

The ache is deep, deep,
deeper.

Deep beneath breastbone, rib,
and blood.
Where sun cannot pierce, and
soul cannot search.
Where the tide rushes out and
the rainwater pools.

The ache is deep, deep,
deeper.

Deep like the echoes that
ravage the halls.
Where voices blend weary and
slippers do not fall.
Where cobwebs cling and
secrets stay buried.

Look in the veil. Look in the
folds. Look over valleys,
mountains, and fields.

No.

Deeper.

Much deeper.

You'll never see deep enough.

The ache is deep, deep,
deeper.

Deep in the woods, over
brambles and thickets.
Where the Fae folk are hiding,
and the toad stools need
riding.
Where children get lost and
there will never be frost.

But—no.

No, no.

The ache is deep, deep,
deeper.

Deep beneath words and
smiles and teeth.
Where nakedness hides and
hopelessness waits.
Deep in the blood, so thick
with distaste.
Where ebony whispers, and
sterling awaits.

Find it there, find it there!

Look closer, look nearer,
reach further, reach longer—

But—but—no...

no...no.

It's deeper. Much deeper.

*The ache is deep, deep,
deeper.*

Weary Bones, Weary Tomes

Did you think I would grow
too weary?
That my knees would shake?
And my knuckles would
bleed?
That my eyes would burn?
And my heart would bound
with need?

Did you think I would give up?
Did you think you would win?
If only you gave me for
another spin?

I am the roar spilling over hill
after hill, racing to the shores.

Broken Boy

I am the scream that fills every
rocky cavern and stream.

Think me weak now?
Think me running and afraid?
Think again, my once dear
friend.

Did you think I would shiver
and shatter?
That the blustering freeze
would be my destruction?
And your wretched words my
abduction?

I am the lion.
I am the bear.
I am your greatest mistake that
you will ever forsake.
I am the case that you can
never erase.

Broken Boy

Did you think your silence
would break bones?
That your cruelty would strip
me bare?
And I would fall to beg for
your mercy?
That your back would sear me
to the core?
And I would come running,
just like before?
Did you think you would win,
if only, you gave me for
another spin?

I cannot die.
For I am anything but a lie.
I cannot be undone.
Try as you might, my once
dear one.

I am the truth spilling over hill
after hill.

Broken Boy

Rushing the shores, with every
ounce of my kills.
I am the scream, that tears
from the throats, from those
who cannot be seen.

Think me weak now?
Think me afraid?

I am the Victory.
I am the Praise.

But I will always, always be
your greatest mistake.
The one you CHOSE to
forsake.

Even so, I am the case, you
can never erase.

I cannot die.
For I am anything but a lie.

Witness

Skin rips on glass. A breath—
one, two.

Crimson seeps, spills, falls.

Tiny slivers of ribbon, tying
knots on skin. Tiny forbidden
secrets, fulfilled by my kin.

A waterfall of fears. Pain
embracing memory.

You watch it pool. You see it
stain.

We lock eyes. You—and I. But
you say nothing.

You do nothing.

For there was never meant to
be a witness, to what aught not
to be done.

In a box, wooden and carved.
Buried—one foot, two.

Fresh earth spread, tilled, laid.

Tiny pieces of souls, tying
worms to the holes. Tiny
forbidden truths, left
suffocating, left dying.

A waterfall of fears. Pain
embracing memory.

You watch it rot. You see the
decay.

We lock eyes. You—and I. But
you say nothing.

You do nothing.

For there was never meant to
be a witness, to the savagery
that's been done.

Heart beating fast inside its
bony cage. Spasm of muscle—
one, two.

Sweaty fingers gripping,
slipping, clawing.

Tiny little screams, too quiet
for ears. Tiny forbidden tears,
black ink burning the
parchment red.

A waterfall of fears. Pain
embracing memory.

You watch it wail. You watch it
writhe.

We lock eyes. You—and I. But
you say nothing.

You do nothing.

For there was never meant to
be a witness, to when
childhood is done.

Naked little creature, so frail
and beaten. Hiding in the
dark. Breathing still—once,
twice.

Limbs quivering, trembling,
breaking.

Tiny little whimpers, reaching
out into the void. Tiny
forbidden secrets, he can never
hope to hide.

A waterfall of fears. Pain
embracing memory.

You watch him scream. You
see him beg.

We lock eyes. You—and I. But
you say nothing.

You do nothing.

For there was never meant to
be a witness, to the inner
creature that is mine.

Skin rips on glass. A
heartbeat—one, two.

Blood drips, slides, falls.

Tiny little whispers, that this is
the last call. Tiny desperations,
that will never make it to the
ball.

A waterfall of fears. Pain
embracing memory.

You turn your back. You close
your ears.

We don't lock eyes. You—and
I. And you say nothing.

You do nothing.

For there was never meant to
be a witness, to what ought not
to be done.

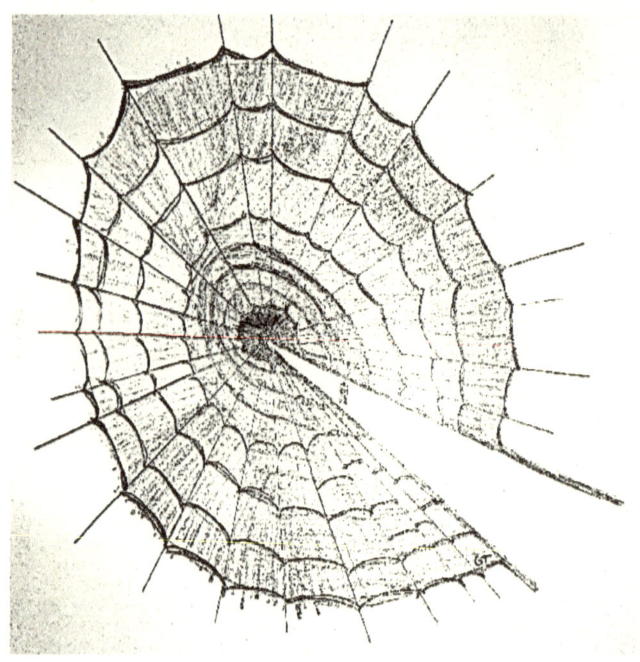

Voices

I can feel their voices in my
head. The sound of screaming
and gnashing of teeth.
Tearing flesh.

The sizzle of fat on hot iron.
Fetid and rank. It fills my
nostrils and I flinch away, body
arching toward light. Any light.
But there isn't any.
The choking filth of smoke
floods over the moors,
suffocating the green,
smudging out the life until
nothing is left.
When I am alone, surrounded
by the darkness, deep in that
familiar dark, ravaged pit, that
is when He comes. That is
where He finds me. Curled in
on myself, naked and
trembling—a frightened little
creature with no senses left to
him.
His hands are cold.
They leave frigid streams down
my cheeks. My spine. My

neck. I lean into the touch, a
desperate animal in need of
contact, completely unaware of
the danger.
I don't notice the wet He
leaves behind.
I don't feel the burn. Or smell
the stench which clings to His
cloaks.
I have been mute for too long.
I have been blind for centuries.
I have been deaf since birth.
Or so it seems.
I go willingly when He takes
my hand and draws me to my
feet. I stumble weakly behind
Him, but I go. I don't fight. I
don't scream when soil turns to
glass and cuts deep into flesh. I
don't break away from Him
when feeling begins to return
and sight and smell follow so

quickly, I am blinking through tears as the image of fire materializes and the scent of death becomes overwhelming.

"Come," His voice is liquid butter, smooth on the tender skin of my cheek as lips of stone brush, kiss, then brush once more.

My knees shake, my ankles lock and I do not come. I do not move.

"Come," He urges once more, those lips feeling more like teeth and that voice becoming tainted with bright sienna anger.

I know where He leads. I know there is only death in His kingdom. But I find my lips moving, and words spilling out of me like hot honey on sweltering concrete.

"Why?"

His nails dig into my skin and I feel the sting down to my marrow. I should run. I should scream. I should do anything but want to cry and fall at His feet with joy. But I have not *felt* in so long. I have not seen or smelled or tasted since before the womb and the want is an infection that only He can cure.

So—when He draws nearer—when He is looking down into my soul with obsidian blood-wet eyes, I don't tear away. I don't even scream. No. I stretch onto tip-toe and welcome His mouth against mine.

I welcome the fire and the heat
and the flame that is His
tongue and lips and teeth. I
welcome the ache and the hurt
and the bitter poison on His
breath. Because my heart is
finally beating. Because
suddenly I am alive and His
mouth, His skin, and His
hands are making it so.
I welcome the end.
Because it is only the
beginning.

Unseen

Weary hands and weary feet
Where does my help come
from?

I stumble wildly in the dark,
reaching for any spark.

From the mountains? The
valleys and hills and streams?
From the tiny voice in the back
of my mind that screams?

Blisters on blisters and blood-
soaked dreams.
I wake frightened and
desperate and far too fatigued.

Where does my help come
from? Where will I find my
relief?

From the oceans? The
deserts? The plains? The skies
high above?
From the crippling confusion
that bellows, 'You are
NOTHING and NO ONE
and certainly not LOVED'?

Micro-fractures in fast brittle
bones.
The heart sinks within its
fleshy tomb.
Lies knit together with lies—
whispering, 'Try harder. Be
better. Or suffer and *die.*'

Where does my help come
from?
Where does it sleep?
Am I forgotten?
Am I forsaken?
Too dirty?
Too deranged?
Has this beloved Lord decided
I am unworthy, too
unchanged?

Or—

Or maybe—

Maybe...as I ask the
unforgiveable, life will become
finally *liveable.*
Maybe as I call out into the
wood, my voice will come back

to me, from the recesses of my
childhood.

Splintered skin and tear-
soaked prayers.
Where does my help come
from?

From God?
From a divine being unfailing
and yet unseen?
From this omnipotent creator
that cannot speak and does not
touch?

Where does my help come
from?
I ask again and again and
again.
But the answer remains.
The truth clear, in silky
refrains.

The man within, shoved into
shadows, struggles forward,
chest lifted, and heart open
wide.
He is naked and thin and
pitifully small.
But his breath still rises, and
his heart still calls.

We lock eyes, he and I, and he
nods—a solemn sigh.

'Me,' we say together, tongue
fat and throat tight.
'Where does my help come
from?'
We whisper it once more.
And this time I answer. The
truth and nothing more.
"Me."

What I Broke

I broke us.
I fell in love and when the love
was gone—
We were too.

I asked for too much.
I needed not enough.
I begged where it was not
wanted.
I broke us.

You said it wasn't my fault.
I lied and said I agreed.
You smiled, I smiled, and the
door closed.
I broke us.

I broke us.
I found where my lines grew.
I cried—and you did too.
You wanted what I couldn't
give.
I wanted what you wouldn't
give.

I broke us.
We were a train headed for the
break in a rail.
And I ended us.
I had no choice—because it was
my voice.
Even as I wished to retract. I
wanted what I lacked.

Because I broke us...but there
is no going back.

MELANCHOLIC DREAMING

He And I

-Rainy Days-

The rain keeps us
indoors—hiding.
We stay in bed. We make
love. We whisper under the
covers and remain within our
nest of naked skin and secrets
till someone's stomach growls.
Then we pad into the kitchen,
barefoot and holding hands to
the tune of thunder rumbling
our ill-fitting windows. The
cabinets rattle with cheap white
dishes and old nick knacks.

Throw pillows are strewn about the living room and there's a bit of leftover Chinese on the kitchen counter. The same photograph of my grandfather on the wall is still crooked and needs fixing. But in this moment, in this quiet breath of grayscale daylight, there is no movement but our own. There is no life, but the one we make of it.

There is only us. There are only these minutes, that lead to moments, that lead to memories. So, we leave it. We don't tidy or clean or plan. After all, it's raining and there is nothing to be done. There should be nothing done. Not today.

I make pancakes, listening to
him humming a Romanian
lullaby that he learned as a boy
and when we sit down to eat,
we decide it would be better to
do it back in our bed. I have
no protests.
The syrup is sticky and it gets
on his chin—on my hands—
then the sheets.
We decide to make love again.
Slower, deeper, more careful
when the rush of need isn't as
strong as the tug for
connection. We wrap around
one another, rocking to that
lullaby he was singing from his
childhood silently in our
minds. Skin against skin, velvet
and crushed cotton. His hands
find mine, our fingers wind
together and we sail over the

edge, one after the next. A great fury of feeling basking in the rainy afterglow of a hot summer thunderstorm.

In between heartbeats, in between breaths, I stare longer than I normally do. I watch his chest rise and fall and take note of the dimple in his cheek. I memorize the band of hazel around the gold of his lion's eyes. I save it. I save it all for the next time we can be like this.

By evening, the sky is a bloated black and we still haven't left our bed. We lie face to face, sharing eyes and breathing space and heat. My skin is so saturated with his that I would smell like him. I do smell like him.

The rain sends us to sleep.
And we don't fight it. I
wrap both arms around him,
nuzzling into the short hair at
his nape and smiling into the
curls that tickle me. His frame
is smaller than mine, bones
thinner, smile wider. But he
fits perfectly against my chest
and every breath he takes, I
take. Every beat of his heart, I
share too. When he drifts off
to sleep and I feel the warm
cadence of his breath on my
forearm, I follow.

-Strawberries-

He tastes like strawberries.
I joke that he could be bottled
and sold as candy and he
smiles at me from across the

kitchen, his dimple flickering and his eyes amused. We share a long look, one tempered by years of knowledge and more quiet looks than one might be willing to count.

Then we go about our nighttime routine.

I make dinner. I'm the better cook out of the both of us and we know it. It's never been an argument. I cook, he does the dishes. I change over the laundry. A fair trade in the books of couples that have been at this for as long as we have.

At the table, he always puts his napkin in his lap and I always lift a mocking brow but say nothing. Habits. Habits that make routines that make our lives. We share our days, telling stories of workplace antics and offering up a few plans for the weekend. We want to visit the local farmer's market and he wants fresh carrots.

Later, when I step into the shower, it doesn't surprise me when he follows.

He presses into the slick skin of my back and wraps his lean arms around my middle. I can feel his nose in my shoulder blades as he inhales, his lips pressing promises into my skin when I stand still and there is the faint, very faint scent of turpentine from the cleaner he uses on his brushes. It lingers with him long after he leaves his studio. Just like his paintings do. They linger in his eyes and his voice. They steal parts of him that I will never be given.

I've learned over the years to make my peace with that.

When I turn, I find his face turned up to mine and his mouth eager. It always is. He never kisses plainly. Never dull. Never without intention and I take full advantage, pressing him into the shower wall and using my size to cage him. He lets me.

He always does.

By unspoken request, I gather the scrubby and soap—strawberry—and lather it into his skin. He lifts his chin for

me and closes his eyes on a
long sigh when I work my way
down his frame. I trace the
lines of his veins with the pads
of my fingers and he laughs
when I tickle his ribs on
purpose. When we rinse, the
strawberry suds go down the
drain and so does the rest of
the weight of our workday.

-Anger-

When he's angry—he yells.
I don't.
I'm not a yeller. I never have
been. I never will be.
But for him, it is an imperative
design. It is the release of
pressure on a valve he has no
hope of controlling and we
both endure it. We have

learned how to avoid it. Or prevent it. But not always. Years do not mean mistakes or humanity disappearing. They do not mean that perfection is achieved and nor should they. We snipe at each other all day. About the chores. About shopping and cooking and everything we never fight about. He's angry with me and short of temper for no apparent reason and when I feel my own patience reaching a boiling point, I walk away. He's so angry. So angry with me.

I don't know why. I'm too angry myself to try and find out why. We separate and go to our own ends of the apartment. Him—to our bedroom. And me, to the spare.

We sit in our stalemate until supper when I emerge and try to salvage the day with a favorite dish. He loves Italian food, but never asks for it. He never asks for many things. It simply isn't how he functions.

He forgets. He daydreams. He—gets lost and then those around him lose track of him as well. They forget him when he is standing right there in the middle of the room.

I try not to.

But sometimes—Gods—sometimes I fail. I fail just like the rest of them.

I start preparing dinner and he comes out to join me. He starts cutting up vegetables for the side. Then he cuts himself. Crimson pours down his hand and he stares at it. No screaming. No sound. Complete stillness and I watch in open shock as he calmly goes to wrap a paper towel around his fingers and then asks me to take him to the ER. Later, much later, when we come home with seven stitches in his ring finger, he tells me that his mother is coming to visit. She insists that she is staying with us in the apartment rather than a hotel. 'Family stays with family.' We've been together for eight years. She has never recognized that he is with me or that I am with him. When

we are in the same room
together, she will not address
me. She will not speak to me.
He hates this. He—has grown
to hate her.
He won't stand up for himself.
I feel my shoulders sag and the
ache I have grown far too
familiar with comes hard and
fast into my middle and I try
not to be angry with him. I try
not to demand he tell her she
isn't welcome in our home.
But I—I can't. I see his face,
weary and exhausted, and then
I see his hand where he sliced
it deep and I think of how this
day has been so very bad and I
do nothing of what I should.
I do nothing really at all.
We climb into bed, I wrap
around him, and we watch TV

with the faint blue glow
spreading over our bed till
neither of us can keep our eyes
open any longer.
In the morning, he calls his
mother. And he tells her she
can't come.
        I hear the words she spits
at him over the line and stop in
the doorway, afraid to move,
let alone breathe. I wait for
him to hang up and for his
head to fall between his
shoulders when he leans into
the counter, then I join him in
the kitchen.
The kiss we share is tainted
with salt. I taste his tears even
as I wipe them away from his
cheeks and whisper how she
doesn't deserve a son like him.

-Sunlight-

On Sundays, we wake before
the sunrise and walk the pier to
see the sun come up over the
water. The wind whips hard off
the bay and it pulls our hair
and jackets. It can be Summer,
or Winter and it is always cold
in San Francisco.
On the bay, it smells like brine
and sea witches. We bring
coffee and drink it black
enough to keep us awake so we
can walk next door to the diner
that's open twenty-four hours a
day. Everything is grease piled
on grease, but we've not
broken this Sunday tradition in
a long, long while.
We watch the sun rise and
climb higher into the sky, an

omen for the day's good fortunes ahead. Or so he tells me. I laugh at his whimsical nature but silently will him to be right. He's never usually wrong about these sorts of things.

We eat breakfast at our diner, and I order the eggs benedict. He always gets French toast smothered in cream. The food tastes more filling than usual so we step out onto the wharf after breakfast and continue our journey deeper into the city. With the brisk jut of the wind, we cling to each other and struggle to keep warm. He laughs when I offer to let him ride piggy-back to the trolley. And then, of course,

takes me up on it. It doesn't
surprise me in the least.
We laugh like loons when I
prance dramatically forward,
and he clings to my shoulders
to stay on. Strangers stare at us.
A couple of tourists offer us
odd looks. I answer their open
perusal of us by stopping to
kiss him deeply on the corner
of Bourbon and Banks. He
opens like a sunflower to me,
his arms winding tightly around
my neck, keeping me bent so
he can reach what he wants,
and I have to stifle a real groan
when he bites my lip and draws
it into his mouth. Whatever
looks we garnered before, are
long gone when we break apart
to breathe.

I'm smiling stupidly the rest of the way home.

I find my smile stays even when we get inside our apartment and he starts stripping out of his clothes, leaving pieces cavalierly in a trail from the doorway to our bedroom. It grows, widening and making my cheeks ache when I follow the trail of clothes and find him standing in the middle of our bed like a warrior with his underwear on top of his head.

I laugh. I laugh so hard my sides hurt and then he's stealing my breath away and his kisses are so urgent, so good and real, that I have to struggle to keep up with him. He is everywhere, fire and sunlight,

doused in the richness of
feeling.

Landing in the middle of the
bed, I stare up at him and feel
lost in his eyes. In that face and
those hands that seek—always
seek for more. He works me
like one of his paintings and it
doesn't take me long to bend
to his whims. I'm a panting
mess by the time he's moaning
and finishing above me. It
takes no more than that to
follow him. Not really. Seeing
him lose himself is enough of a
reward.

After, amidst sweat-damp
sheets and a boneless man
weighing me into the mattress,
I realize he's still wearing the
underwear on his head. I pluck
at the waistband and he jerks

as it snaps on his forehead.
Then laughter bubbles up
beside me, throaty and light—
with reckless abandon. And it
sounds like sunlight.

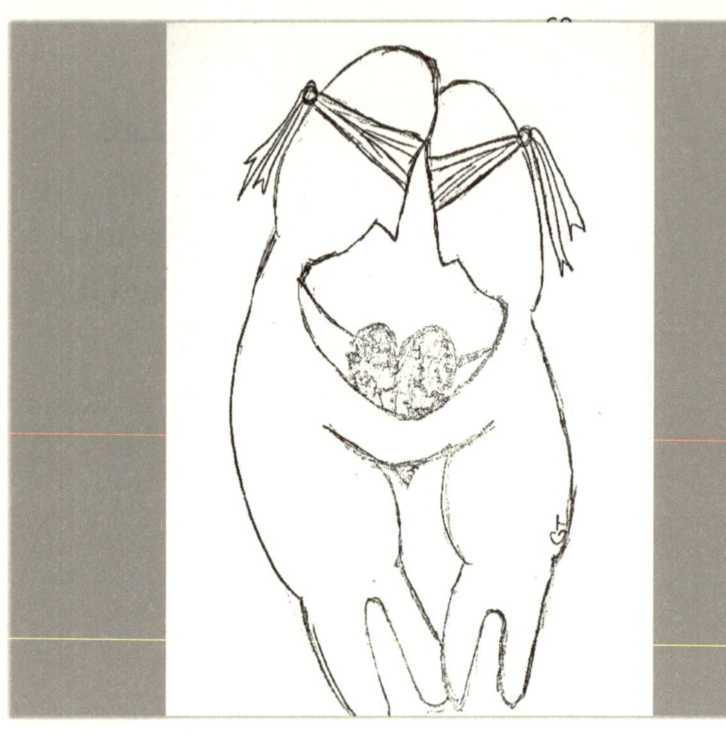

Angel

Do you know your worth,
Angel?

Do you see the light that pours
from you like water in the
falls?

Black ringlets dressed in silver
ribbon. Sapphire and baby
pink and cream. Small hands.
Small toes. Biggest heart.

Do you watch the moon,
Angel, like I watch it? Willing
it nearer? Bidding it closer?

Do you bask in the sunlight
and garner its power? For the
bitter months and the long
hours and the darkness which
hides.

Do you think of me Angel?

As I think of you?

Abalone wishes in moonstone
thoughts. Gossamer dreams

that tease and touch. Soft skin.
Softer lips. Softest heart.

Do you run with your arms
open wide and your eyes to the
sky?

Do you cry when the night
steals the light?

Do you imagine ebony flowers
and rain-soaked leaves?

Spring and Autumn. Winter
and Summer. Seasons drifting
into seasons. Their lazy fingers
tugging lovers nearer and
hearts closer.

Broken Boy

Do you see me, Angel? Do you see *this* heart? That burns and froths and begs where it should not?

Do you see these scars? These tears and these marks?

My dearest Angel, they are yours and yours alone. Every craggy little stone. Every time when I am alone.

Do you know your worth, Angel?

Do you see the gravity that tugs and binds?

The thread of silver to the vines?

Dew drops cling to roses'
petals. Pads of fingers,
touching beckoning,
calling...more, More.

MORE.

Do you hear the siren's wail?
Far above my own stormy gail?
It screams, 'Angel! Angel!
Where are you, Angel?!'

Dawn brings stillness—the grip
of death like fair kisses to
cheeks, the brush of knuckles
and skin, the dark touch of
needs unmet.

Are you here Angel? Am I still
alone?

Are you here?

Do you see the stars so far
above, hiding like children
behind their velvet gloves?

Do you feel the pull that drives
us up onto our toes?

Do you see me calling, Angel?

Mouth open, hands wide,
chest lifted. Every fiber
abandoned. Every pore
braced.

Are you here, Angel? Can you
see me?

Wheat fields and wisps of
white. Tearstains shrouding the
bloodred sight.

Broken Boy

Am I breathing?

Is this worthless heart still
beating?

Are you even real?

Perhaps. Maybe. Possibly.

Do you know your worth,
Angel? Can you even fathom?

Not nearly.

Not ever.

And so, it will be never be.

Broken Boy

I Used To Remember

I used to remember what
fingers felt like tracing skin
I used to remember the brush
of lips on cheek
the tickle of beard on neck
the rush of falling with no
ledge

I used to remember it—
And remember it well.

I held the memories tight to
chest
my grip unfailing and the best
I didn't think I could lose it
Not ever.
Not really.

I used to remember what being
held while I slept felt like

Broken Boy

I used to remember the hush
of morning,
the secret of skin on skin,
the rapid thrum of twin pulses
excited by love

I used to remember it—
And remember it so. damn.
well.

But I loosened my grip
I let them slip
One by one, they shriveled
without care until it was more
than I could bear

I used to remember another
His spirit and mine so tightly
wound, one could not tell up
from down.

Broken Boy

I used to remember how to
feel, but then it became real—
so, so real.

And I was alone.
The room was too big for me,
and me alone.

And I realized—I realized I
forgot...
I forgot what maybe I should
not.

I used to remember.

I held the memories inside my
chest, and I thought they
would never leave me, like all
of the rest.

I used to remember what eyes
peering into soul was like,

Where heart beat into heart.
And lovers were born like a
piece of art.

I used to remember the smell
of soft flannel
The taste of another's skin
The hidden places no one
could lay claim

I used to remember it.
And I—I remembered it well.

Meadow Beast

Look deep into the grayish
light
Over rocky knolls and shrubby
blight.
Beyond the veil where night
creeps to night
And deep beneath the rare
blooms bright.

There lives a creature, so quiet
and warm.
Though there be not any who
can recall his true form.

Blades of grass—pressing and
yearning.
Whispering and laughing.
They speak of the meek and
tell tales of the mild.

Their voices carry higher and
higher...beyond any of that in
the wild.

Look far below that bloated
sun
Over naked boughs and
broken branches.
Past the trickling tongues
where the rivers meet—to
where Elvin make magic
though their hymns be quite
tragic.

There lives a beast, so soft and
forlorn
His minky coat not shiny but
clearly quite shorn.
Lightning bugs dither, rushing
to and fro. Zipping and
zapping.
And all but flapping.

They sing of the weary.
They chant of the mild.
Their voices carry higher and
higher...beyond any of that in
the wild.
Look long into the meadow
child.
Longer than Summer or even
the Fall, longer than dew drops
that creep at a crawl.
Longer still, until you feel ill
and then—then you will see
why.

The Meadow Beast will not
come, but only for a beat. For
a pause.

And certainly with no claws.

Broken Boy

His eyes will search wide and
then very, very deep.
His words will be gentle and
cast you fast, fast asleep.

In your dreams he will follow,
where the heart is not hollow.
In laughter he will cling, so that
he might sing.
There, only there, can the
Beast truly be seen.

Look deep into the meadow's
light
Through fog in the bog,
through the green that's rather
mean.
Over sunflowers and
toadstools.
Past earth and needle and
pine.

Broken Boy

There lives a Beast, so tired
and worn.

Though there be not any, who
have seen his true form.

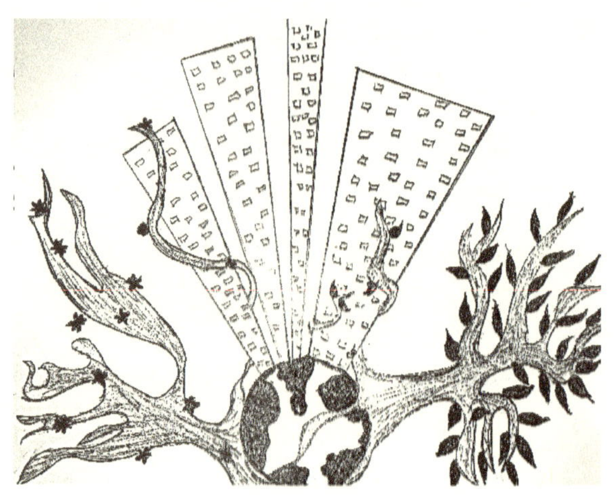

Do The Trees Cry?

Do trees cry when we cut
them?
Does the ocean moan as it fills
with our trash and blackens
like ink spilling on fresh snow?

Do the birds look forlorn as
they soar over our jungles of
concrete and steel?

I asked a Cardinal once as it
landed in my yard if he grew
weary of the humans who
sullied his home—
He chirped. He ate his full. He
flew off after a shared stare of
glossy black to faded blue.
Was his answer the silence?
Or was he too busy to notice
another fleshy mammal
disrupting his breakfast?

Do the fish whine that they die
in our plastic?
Do the deer scream when they
run from our guns or see a
flash of hunters orange?

Broken Boy

Does the wind choke when it
fills with our smoke?

I keep asking—but they just
keep staring. But I suppose
that's an answer in itself

2020

Breath in. Breath out.
I watch my chest rise and fall
in a half-baked sun and I
wonder when my day will
come.
When this chest will rise with
sacred air no longer.

Breath in. Breath out.
My heart squeezes in my chest
I feel the heat of skin beneath
my palm. I close my eyes and
wonder how awful it would feel
to have that steady heavy
beat...stop.

Breath in. Breath out.

The shell of my hear presses
down on his chest, my son's
snoring breaths are like music
and I fall asleep with a prayer
tumbling from my lips, even as
I don't believe.

Breath in. Breath out.
I watch the news, my mask
tight to my nose. I can smell
laundry detergent, antiseptic,
and my home. I worry that I
won't keep them all safe and I
struggle not to panic.

Breath in. Breath out.
I see the signs at the store, the
limitations of quantity, the
empty shelves
I grab the shopping cart tighter,
my lungs burning and I sip my
air until I leave

Broken Boy

Breath in. Breath out.
The snow comes and we still
hide our children.
The government is a mockery
and the snow dampens our
fears
We shop. We dress the walls
in color. But I measure my
heartbeats and watch my wife
do the same.

Breath in. Breath out.
It's six seconds to midnight.
The air is like glass.
We watch with our eyes wide
and our hearts in our throats.
The clock strikes the new year
and we all start to cry.
I pull down my mask and for
the first time, I breathe clear.

When She Wakes Up

There is a moment before she
first wakes, that I feel the entire
world around us, a steady
pressure of heated flesh and
coppery blood. I lean into the
feeling, pressing my cheek
hard into the cold sheets and I
wait. I wait for it to pass. I wait
for the clock to keep ticking
and the world to glance away—
fastidiously ignoring my
existence as it always has.
In that pause—I fear losing her
the most.

I fear what and who and why
and where I am.
I fear the very breath in my
lungs and the pulse that
bounds in my ears.
I fear she will turn, glance in
my direction and realize what
she is lying next to and then it
will be done. Like snapping
dry twigs between a finger and
thumb, she will crumble before
me. A mirage that fades out of
my arms, leaving nothing, not
even her warmth.
The feeling always passes. The
clock keeps going. The world
looks away. The room
breathes a sigh of relief and the
pressure beneath my ribcage
loosens with fatigue.
The end never comes.

But just before she wakes,
before her eyes flutter and her
lashes fan dark on her
cheekbones, I wonder if today
is the day that I am wrong.

Silliness

it's silly really
how often my mind wanders
and strays
how the reeds bend in the
breeze
while the cogs lock up—and
freeze
it's silly really

it's silly really
how i think of you
how it goes back on its own
like retracting within my home
it's silly really

Broken Boy

it's silly really
how i know you won't come
how i feel you are long gone
but i wait at the door
like i do when i'm sure
it's silly really

Dark

Dark is the shroud that clouds
my eyes.
Dark is the feeling that pours
between your lies.

Light

Light is the kiss that brushes
my skin.
Light is the feeling that floods
into my sins.

I Still

I still love Them.
Maybe more than I did the last
time we met, and we were
sitting in this shared space of
paper with coffee perfuming
the air. Air conditioning hums
over the vents and there They
are—soft, unassuming and
gentle. A delicate flower left
ragged by the world that
doesn't deserve Them. I watch
Them, knowing deep in my
gut, that I would make Them
happy.
I stare too long. I want too
much. I need—It doesn't

matter what I need. Not really. Not now.

This isn't about all that. It is enough to sit a handspan apart and see Them beside me. With me. It is enough to smell the lavender oil on Their skin and to admire the threads of silver in Their hair. It's enough to know that I am someone special to Them. That I matter to this human who has stolen far more than just my friendship.

I know there will be days I want more.

There are already days that I do.

I want to wake up in the morning to Them in the bed beside me. I want to share the same space as Them. Live in

Their towers of books and
whisper secrets late at night. I
want to shelter Them from the
storm and worry about Their
fears for Them.
I want and I want and I want.
I CAN'T have, what is not
offered or will ever be.
They are the sort to stay with
someone till death do them
part. They are the loyal sort.
The same beautiful things that
I love about Them now, will
also make Them impossible to
have. Even in the future. And
in truth, can any person really
have another? Can they ever
really possess a human being
as if they are an object?
The answering is simple. And
yet, blisteringly painful.
Of course not.

They will leave this place and go back to Their husband and children. They will go back to Their problems and Their life and Their comforts and I will go back to mine. I'll think of Them often and I will force myself to care a little less. I will force myself to not daydream of what Their lips might feel like on my own.
Of what Their hands would be like to hold and the lines in Their palms would feel like to trace.
I ache to touch Their hair. To wind those unruly auburn curls around my fingers. I ache to rub the kinks from Their shoulders and to kiss the fears far, far, away.

I wish, more than I ever, ever should. And I wonder, if one day, will this deep yearning ever end? Or am I setting myself up for a lifetime of pining the likes of which will consume me till I become nothing but a needy mess of want?

I can't say.

And honest to the gods, I don't really want to know. Why would I? It will only hurt me.

I'm certain of that much.

Run, run, as fast as I can, but I will never outrun my feelings for this person. I will never stop thinking about Them as more than just a friend. I will never stop wanting Them as more than just my family.

HOPEFUL WHIMSY

Look At You

When I look at you,
I feel your lips on the shell of
my ear,
Your breath a promise,
Your fingertips a question

I lean in—eyes fluttering closed,
body all yours and yours alone

And you take my answer with
lips and teeth and tongue

I see verdant on honey
Your lashes brushing abalone,
Your veins a steady river,
Taking you straight to home

Broken Boy

You press in—nose to neck,
teeth to blood, tongue to bone

Yearning becomes burning and
I let you throw me on the pyre

When I look at you,
I hear a pulse,
Drumming in my ears,
Thrumming in my core,
Humming for just one more

We grab on—diving deep to
silence it all, succumbing to a
velvet darkened world

Body into body and breath
into breath
There is no two but one
A wild web we've just begun

When I look at you, I see me.

A soul matching soul.
A body reveling in body.
A home seeking home.

Making Love

When we make love, he
likes his hands in my hair,
great fistfuls of it.
His mouth finds the
sensitive skin of my nape and
he nibbles, his lips sending
gooseflesh all down my frame.
I arch into him, the ridges of
my spine pressing like pearls
into the hot skin of his belly.
He groans.
Always does. Seemingly
set aflame by witnessing my
earnest enjoyment—paralyzed
by the wickedness of such a
strong body submitting and

then becoming naked clay to
another in those long artist
hands of his.
His skin never leaves
mine. Not for a moment. Not
for a breath.
When we fall, we fall
together.

She And I

-A Bud-

She keeps a rose I gave
to her pressed between glass
on her nightstand. The petals
are crushed pink and yellow, a
sunset of a memory one
summer ago. I remember
sitting in the grass, digging out
weeds to the hum of insects
with the sun warming my skin.
I'd felt soft and nostalgic—
peaceful with soil under my
nails and woodchips digging
into my shins. By the time I'd
started pruning the roses, my

thoughts had already drifted to her.

Those pixie cheekbones and soft slender hands. Long silken hair and dark wise eyes.

When I close my eyes, I can smell the lotion on her skin.

I remember cutting a single perfect bud, twisting the thorny stem between my fingers, entranced by its singular beauty. I immediately thought of giving it to her. Of leaving the tiny offering on her pillow, pressing a kiss to her temple, and then sneaking away before dawn. She would smile and I wouldn't have to be there to know it would be a sight as lovely as the rose bud.

Bright and unassuming and pleased. Soft.

She kept the flower, as I knew she would, and immediately framed it—forever memorializing a perfect summer moment. Capturing the mundane to make it magical. A gift she seems to only be perfecting as we age.

I see her staring at it on rainy days, tucking her hair behind an ear, petite bare feet pressed into chilly wood flooring. Her expression is always thoughtful and as deep as the lake to the west of our property.

If I ask her what she is thinking of, it is always the same.

She turns, my favorite
smile crinkling the corners of
her eyes, and she says, "You."

-Banana Bread-

On Sunday mornings, she
makes banana bread with great
big chunks of walnuts.
I can smell it from the
bedroom, wafting through our
vents like a lover's caress from
nose all the way down to my
toes.
She always comes back to bed
after putting the bread into the
oven, hair tied back into a
sloppy bun, hands smelling
like fresh fruit and cinnamon.
She never fails to be wearing
one of my shirts—Spongebob
or Metallica. Something ratty

and barely wearable, but soft and familiar. And she will never be wearing anything underneath. Nothing but skin and secrets, a promise of what she might give me if I am only willing to ask.

There is something comical and yet unabashedly sensual about knowing she has been baking in our kitchen like that. Nearly naked. But not quite. The knowledge never ceases to drive me just a bit wild. Unlocking some sort of feral caveman need to possess and taste and touch. To have as much as she will let me as quick as she will let me. To map her freckles with my tongue and imprint the feeling into my hands into her soul.

I suspect she is fully aware of
what those ratty t-shirts do to
me while she bakes her banana
bread. And that is precisely
why she does it.
She'll usually taste like coffee
and in between kisses I tell her
so—chastising her for not
bringing me a cup while curling
a hand into hair to keep her
mouth captive to mine. The
ocher of those summer-kissed
eyes will narrow behind heavy
lids and the need always builds
to a fever pitch. So much I
ache. Kissing her pulse
produces a keening request
that I stutter to answer. It
makes my belly hollow and my
hands shake. Coltish and
shaky, I murmur nonsensical
promises into her damp skin,

unable to stop my mouth from running ahead of my body.
But she arches into my words, a desperate sweetness clinging to the air, rushing us on. When she bites her lip, looking at me with those fathomless witch's eyes, as if I am her deity and her Sunday morning banana bread was her offering, I come undone.
We make love in a rushed haze.
When we surface, there is usually only minutes to spare before the timer on the oven goes off. The whole house will smell like fresh-baked bread and it makes the minutes following our coupling more ethereal. More like a dream than reality.

Broken Boy

I don't know how we manage
to have unburned banana
bread every week.
But we manage.
I bring platefuls of steaming
bread back to bed, smothered
in butter, and we feast like
heathens in bed, lying in the
sunlight pouring in from our
windows. It is my favorite day
of the week.

Windchimes, Bird Song, and Sirens

We step outside like
frightened roaches.
Afraid of the balm of sunlight
and fresh air. Afraid of the
chorus of birds that ribbon
overhead.
Our eyes search the fence line,
wary and aimless.
Alert for the invisible predator
we know to be in our midst.

Minutes tick by.
Fingers loosen.

Hearts slow.
Breaths...linger.

There is a warmth at dusk—
shadowed secrets and pixie
hollow dreams.
Reality fades to grayscale and
the night swarms into the void.
It overwhelms with its sights
and sounds and smells.
Fresh-cut grass fills the nose as
the breeze tugs at those sun-
bleached wooden chimes.

The world forgets.
A moment.
A hush.
And we settle in.

We burrow into our seats, eyes
round and child-like, though
no children can be heard.

We don't hear the sounds of
fighting, the echoing wail of a
dog left on its chain or the
bleeding cry of those sirens
which come night or day.
We can't see the garbage in the
ally or lined along the street.

Minutes slide past.
Muscles go soft.
Bones don't ache.
The soul sighs.

My hands smell like bleach
and antiseptic, but I only smell
the dirt freshly damp in the
flower beds.
I tug my sweater tighter, but I
don't feel the chill.
The sun has dipped beyond
view, taking with it the last bits
of light.

But the flicker of a candle and
a shared smile brightens our
square of yard for miles.

There is no death toll.
No masks.
No gloves.
No exhausted, withering, tales.

There is only spring and the
valiance of life going on.
Our presence is not needed,
but we witness it just the same.
We keep quiet, the stars
struggle into view, and a tiny
red beetle lands on my thumb.
I like the company and my
mouth hitches up—a smile
without strings, with no need to
try.

We stay long.

Broken Boy

Drinking up our fill.
Bodies fully lax.
Minds like the bees that got
into too much honey.

But it ends. It always does.
The doors beckon at our backs
and the sirens rush us all along.
We retreat within our home.
Bones encased in cement with
hearts that remember to sprint.
The walls are warm and safe—
but we cannot feel it.
We peer outside the windows,
and see the spell is done.

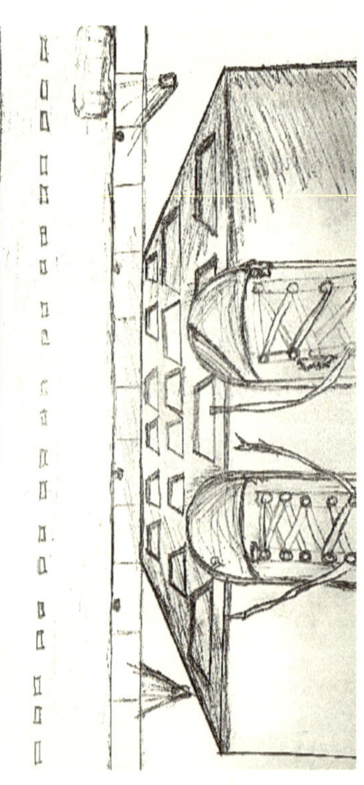

Samuel

For Connor

One.
You are a daisy burning bright
in the fields. Stumbling and
playing, with no end in sight.
You don't know, nor could
you ever, that this is the start of
a very long plight.
I don't know you, and I won't
just yet.
I am too young.
We've only just met.

Five.
You swing your legs and watch
the screen, letters and numbers
and black and white.
You smile, you listen, you look
up and think I can fly—
I do my best, but I don't see
you.
I barely even try.

Seven.
You copy my movements and
learn very fast. I share some
secrets and we try hard to
laugh.
You get smarter, you get faster,
and you still think that I fly.
I do my best, I really do.
But I still don't know why.

Ten.
You build worlds and your
heart is like fire. We hide in
the letters and the numbers
and the black and the white.
You bleed darker, you slip
deeper, but you still reach out
and try.
I do my best, even though I am
like all the rest.
Because I am barely alive.

Thirteen.
You learn to survive, you
become like a kite, the strong
arm of love, barely keeping
you from flight.
You struggle, you scream, and
you cry but you still reach out
in search of that line.

I do my best, but I fear I am
like the rest.
Because I am nearly out of
time.

Seventeen.
You become brazen, you
speak, and you climb. I
stumble behind you, too weak
for your side.
You smile, you listen, and you
still tell me that I can go
higher.
I do my best, because you
deserve nothing less.
But I become like all the rest.
And I fear this is a test.

Nineteen.
You fall. The deep pit of black
swallows up over your head
and I watch in horror, mouth

sewn shut and hands bound
tight.
You weep, you break, and I
desperately tell you that you
can still fly.
I do my best, because you
need me to make your nest.
And I brace for the shame.
Because I should have called
your name.

Twenty.
You hold my hand, you tell
truth, and you dare to breathe.
You ask me to follow and I
take your lead.
You laugh again, you cry but
we are free. You still remind
me that together we can never
die.
I do my best, because I finally
believe that it is enough.

Broken Boy

And we bare our souls.
Because we cannot live without
being whole.

My Charles

I wake before dawn and still
smell your skin on the sheets
The dust moats hum with our
muted laughs and the sun
streams harbor the secrets we
make last.
When I roll, arm reaching, I
don't find soft skin and bone.
But I don't realize I am alone.

We banter over breakfast and
dance naked after dishes.

Broken Boy

I tell you that you're funny and
you manage to tease me into a
blush.
The kiss we share is as warm as
the fleece sweater I tug on for
the day.

Your innocence burns away
the fog on the bay, and we play
like children until noontime
tides threaten us away.

When I grin and cuddle closer
to you after supper, I don't
find soft skin and bone.
I still don't realize that I am
alone.

The fire crackles along to my
sleepy renditions of Austen
and Poe.

I read out loud and you listen
with that smirk—the one that
says you could do better and
we both know that you could.

At eight, the house groans like
the age in my bones and I
blink in the grainy dim. I
imagine a face that I know as
well as my own.
"Happy 80th, baby," you
whisper and the hush that
follows is not unwelcome or
sewn.

When I stretch out a hand, to
trace a line, a forehead, a brow,
I don't find muscle or tissue or
bone.
I don't care that I am most
certainly alone.

"Goodnight, my Charlie," I
whisper back, my throat tight
and voice so thin.
When you hum back, your
ageless tenor a brush of skin, I
close my eyes.

In our dreams, I am never
alone.

A Name

My name is irrelevant
A sound with syllables
And broken spaces

Pauses with breaths...

But it is my name

And it belongs to ME.

A medallion of sage imprinted
with letters,
The syllables

The broken spaces

The...breaths.

And it belongs to ME.

Believer

You make me believe that time
is forgiving
Crinkles on skin
Ink blots on paper
Screams in a void
Blood-stained knees
It can all be undone

Clock hands can skip
backward
Porcelain can un-fracture
Tender kisses can bandage
bruises
And whispered promises can
mend all wounds

Broken Boy

You make me believe that the
years are just a memory
Old tears in pages
Scarred knuckles
Cold sweat-soaked dreams
Brittle cruelty in words
It can all be undone

You say the darkness can fade
Green sprouts after pain
Acceptance can smother
hatred
And lips soaked in honey
bewitch even the darkest of
demons

You make me believe that I
was never lost
Barefoot and broken by the
frost
Wet cheeks

Broken Boy

Struggling and frightened
breaths
Absent
It can all be undone

Comfort can be offered, you
say
Comfort can be taken, you
remind
The body can mend
The soul can revive
The mind can move on

You make me your believer
And I gladly fall in love

Sea Foam

In the space between waking
and sleeping
he waits for her

Where the moon drips her
tears
Like all of his fears
And they press together
In a bed of pale heather

He holds his breath and hears
the darkness creep.

He holds his breath and waits
for the deep.

Broken Boy

Her seafoam fingers caress
Like the waves meeting at
shoreline
And they press together,
A lost soul and a lover

He holds his breath and hears
his darkness fleeing
He holds his breath and
waits for it to keep

I Fell In Love

I fell in love with her when we were children. I remember the exact moment, like the afterburn in a flash photograph.
We had mud squishing between our toes like hot tar as we crashed through the swamps. Trodding into murky water where tadpoles and crawdads threatened the sanctity of our baby-skinned ankles. Sun-warmed and sticky with sweat, we painted our cheeks with black paint and caught dragonflies like we were

hunting monsters in the
Amazon jungle.
You were my dark moon and I
was your sun. We revolved
around each other—gravity
pulling and binding us
together.
We were up to our thighs in
the brackish pond, laughing
like loons when I realized it.
I saw her eyes looking deep
into mine, past the surface into
the vulnerable tender bits, the
places I had not even learned
to like about myself yet. And I
knew.
I loved her.
Ten years later, stirring a cup
of burnt sienna tea and
watching her glow as she spoke
of theater and flowers and
dreams—I was struck again.

She was soft edges and lines.
Vulnerability in an ivory
package. I knew I wanted her
then, just like I knew I would
never be able to voice those
words.
Not then.
I didn't think I could ever.
But fast forward five years—she
is leaning against a wall, her
eyes lost and weary, face drawn
and broken. I am so quiet
because I don't know what to
say. I can't make this better. I
have no words for her now
either. But I want to close the
seams in her world that are
bursting, the ragged threads all
but destroyed.
I know it now. I know I am still
in love with her, just like when
we were children and we

dreamed of Fae folk stealing us away. I know it now, watching her eyes fill with tears in the harsh light of a hospital, when the doctor tells her it's done. Her father passed on.

I take her hand and she clings so tightly the bones in my hand ache like the heart in my chest. But my mouth feels dry and I can't say it. My eyes burn and I look away.

I fell in love with her so long ago, so many years layered upon years and memories that I don't remember a day when I was not in love. I don't know if I could keep living and breathing without it.

When I follow her into the cab, she takes my hand and

brushes a kiss on my cheek.
My mouth opens, closes, then
opens again and nothing
comes out.
I still can't say it. So, I
don't.
But I think she sees it.
I hope she knows.
Because I fell in love
with her when we were
children and I never grew up.

Freckles
For Samantha

I found my lucky rabbit's foot
on your elbow and the sun on
your shoulder blade.
Sweat peas on vines, that lulled
along your spine.
A half moon, a wolf crying, the
horizon on a wave
I found them hiding on your
skin. I found them when I
grew brave.

I traced butterflies into your
lips and hearts on your cheeks.

Tiny pathways leading into sin,
tiny flowers layered into skin.
A star, a blueberry, a lion who
had won.
I found them hiding on your
skin. I kissed them all and
came undone.

I told my secrets to the maiden
who lived so gently on your
neck.
Speckled cats, sleeping soundly
on your lats
A stolen kiss, a screaming
wind, the pearl within a wreath
I found them hiding on your
skin. I marked them soft
between my teeth.

I found my heart within your
freckled stars, and my breath
within your spin

Chocolate drops and witchy
spells. They graced your
shoulders, hips, and swells.
A galaxy, a comet, a sprinkle of
rare moon dust
I memorized them on your
skin. I pressed my heart into
their trust.

I close my eyes and see them
still.
Freckles upon freckles, like a
dream of patchwork frills.
A beginning with no end, a kiss
that lingers, a heart that wakes
I found them hiding in your
love. A spotted forest for my
aches.

Broken Boy

Broken Boy

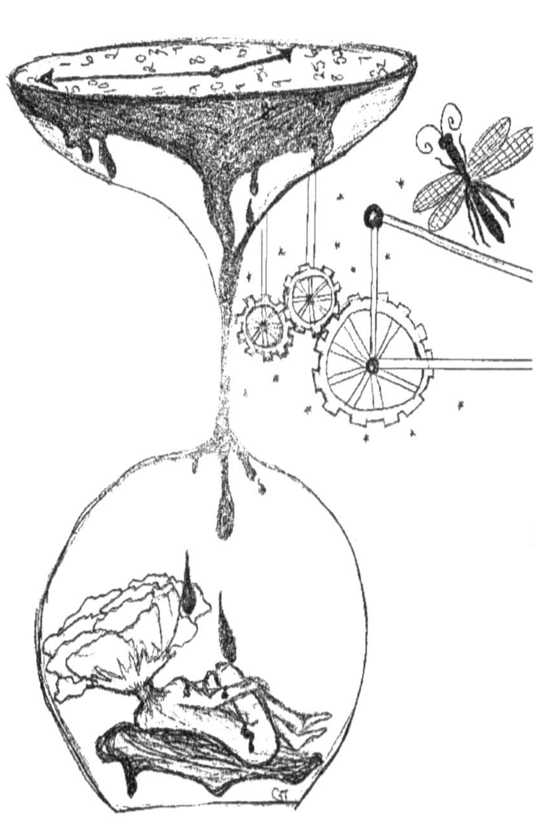

Wrinkles

They hide laughs, little hidden
pennies in a tear drop
They seal memories in a quiet
feathering mirror
Delicate webs of kisses at the
corners of eyes
Angling a mouth, pressing an
upper lip, tattooing a temple

They map the stones of
decades stacked one over the
other
They sprinkle anecdotes and
words of wisdom

Spiraling soft snapshots into
knuckles
Life lessons into knees, and
silken secrets into napes

The crows feet beneath
makeup, the laugh lines that go
deep
The worry furrow
The drape of old age
The delicate paper of skin
born witness to another age

Wrinkles, crinkles, and creases
Lines with a thousand stories
we forget to remember
A path oft taken, if only we
look
They are the visible secret no
soul is without.

Fin

Acknowledgements

I would like to thank my beautiful wife for her constant support and for inspiring so many of my poems.

Thank you to my brother Connor, for being my partner in crime and never ceasing to cheer me on.

Thank you to all my kiddos— you three make my world go round.